CW00686764

Staff and Educational Development Association

Using Varied Media to Improve Communication and Learning

Chris O'Hagan
University of Derby

SEDA Special No. 4
July 1997
ISBN 0 946815 69 0

Preface

This is a completely rewritten book rather than a revision of its antecedent - Using Audio Visual Aids Creatively. However, I would like to acknowledge the help that gave me as a loose guide, and which made the task a lot easier than working ab initio. So, many thanks are due to Kate Ashcroft, Graham Gibbs, David Jacques and Chris Rust of Oxford Brookes University for this; but even more thanks are due to them from all those relative newcomers to teaching in higher education who for eight years have found the inspiration and the confidence to use educational media from within the pages of Using Audio Visual Aids Creatively. I only hope that this replacement will be as useful to its readers - to the ultimate benefit of all our students.

I have tried to balance general advice with technical advice and with some simple suggestions for use in teaching and learning which a lecturer relatively new to teaching should be able to accommodate into his or her practice relatively quickly and with the kind of technical support available in most higher education institutions. I also include a few ideas which need a bit more experience or more complex technical support, but I have tried not to overdo this aspect despite the general trend to technology-assisted learning, and despite the risk of seeming not quite up-to-date. The intention is to provide a practical understanding of a range of media, (and I am sure that even the experienced lecturer will find something useful). Armed with this understanding I hope teachers will find many other effective ways of using educational media suggested by other books in the SEDA Specials series and by their own experience.

Each Chapter has a KEY or KEYs with which I seek to encapsulate something of the essence of the media discussed. I have collated these KEYS together with the Contents to provide a quick overview. You may freely copy these two pages to give to staff - it may help direct them to this volume if they do not have a copy, or act as an aide memoire if they do.

Chris O'Hagan
July 1997

The Author is Head of the Centre for Educational Development and Media at the University of Derby. He is also Director of the Derby Centre of the Teaching and Learning Technology Support Network, which provides free consultancy and support to higher education institutions in the UK. Chris is pleased to offer advice on or clarification of anything in this publication.

C.M.OHagan@derby.ac.uk or tltsn@derby.ac.uk
www.derby.ac.uk/cedm/welcome.html

The Graphic Artist for the illustrations is Steve Hodson,
Centre for Educational Development and Media, University of Derby.

Contents and Keys to Success

Note: Multiple copies of the "Contents and Keys to Success" pages may be made for staff development purposes provided the source is acknowledged on each copy. This permission excludes any commercial use.

Chapter 1: Audiovisual Aids, Out; Educational Media, In

I have deliberately avoided using the expression 'audiovisual aids' in the title of this booklet. Apart from the fact that it sounds a bit old-fashioned in this computer age (though without doubt the computer is an audiovisual medium) it also suggests that slides, videorecordings etc. are dispensable 'aids' to teaching and learning - that they are not at the centre, but are a kind of icing on the cake.

It is true, 'audiovisual aids' are often treated in this way - useful for illustration, for a bit of reinforcement, as a stimulus to discussion - and not as integral to the processes of communication and the facilitation of student learning. However, there is substantial evidence that simultaneously engaging eye and ear in the learner can improve comprehension and retention, that visual structures like charts and diagrams can help the development of mental structures, that helping students to think and analyse visually is as important as helping them to think and analyse verbally.

In other words, when you are preparing teaching or learning materials, you should ask, "How can I visualise the verbal, and how can I verbalise the visual?" At a simple level this may be preparing overhead projector transparencies for a lecture which use patterns of key words to exemplify the structure behind the discussion, or helping students discuss a news photograph or an X-Ray slide. At a more sophisticated level it might be a student project to develop a storyboard for a video programme on a particular issue, or analysing how the movie with Mel Gibson as Hamlet has cut the original text by using the powers that film has over stage presentation.

But let us not forget that the expression educational media brings in methods which do not automatically come to mind with the word audiovisual - handouts and booklets, flip charts, whiteboards, computer-based learning.

You as a teacher are an exemplar to your students of the effective communicator. Effective use of the tools available to you is not just a measure of how effectively you will communicate, but will also help guide your students towards becoming effective communicators themselves.

KEY: Integrate educational media into your teaching and your students' learning. Visualise the verbal, and verbalise the visual.

Chapter 2: Hints and Tips for the Successful Use of Media

A whole range of factors can affect the effectiveness of materials and their use.

Fitness for Purpose:

The use of educational media has been seriously set back by misguided notions of quality, with the imperatives that producers should try to emulate commercial values e.g. glossy brochures in print or broadcast TV in video. The standard of production should fit the designated purpose. There is no point in wasting precious resources on higher than necessary production values. A handout in a lecture may be simple, produced on a photocopier in 300 dots per inch (dpi). Even published academic books are often produced to standards below those of the mass market because sales do not justify higher quality. Very high quality production often signals the 'coffee table' book - entertaining but superficial.

In higher education we may wish to actually avoid signs of conspicuous expenditure because they signal low intellectual expectations. This is no better exemplified than in video. The exhortation to equal broadcast standards is in my view one of the reasons why video is not more widely used. In higher education the last thing we should aim at is imitating the aura of TV in the domestic lounge: it signals passivity, entertainment (or at best 'edutainment'), and intermittent attention. Too often educational video producers have been seduced to lower intellectual content in order to be more 'entertaining'. Understandably, they don't want to be accused of being boring, but perhaps I am alone in admiring those early Open University TV programmes! A generation of mature students found intellectual identity through them. They were fit for purpose, and probably much better than the average live university lecture at that time.

KEY: Focus on effective communication, not surface production values. Fitness for purpose means it is readable, audible, clearly presented and, of course, appropriate.

Teaching rooms:

Know your room and its facilities. Check windows for suitable blinds; check screens and equipment. If you can vary the position of facilities, work out optimum positioning for visibility, and how you will work round the equipment. Try not to put the equipment between you and your audience - you will communicate better if you can move out in front of it. If you have to use a microphone, ask for a radio microphone so that you have mobility and are not confined behind a lectern. Be careful you do not personally obstruct your audience's sight lines to screens etc: stand to the side, sit down, or move around.

Lighting:

Make sure you can raise and lower lights effectively. If you have to lower lights so that projection equipment is bright enough, try to ensure enough ambient lighting remains so that students can see to take notes. Raise the lights as soon as you can: don't work for long periods in dim lighting. Apart from eye strain causing loss of concentration in your students, you will lose eye contact with your audience (or the illusion of eye contact in large venues). Quite simply, you will communicate more effectively and better retain student attention in a well-lit room. Eye strain will be worst if the ambient lighting is brighter than the image on the screen: hence the need to control lights and provide breaks where students are not required to look at a screen, but at a well-lit 'you'.

KEY: Keep in 'contact' with your audience. Don't hide behind equipment, keep the lighting bright and keep eye contact when you want to hold the attention rather than your resources.

Equipment:

Try to ensure it is in good working order, and that you know the location and function of the controls you will need. However, you will inevitably encounter malfunctioning equipment. Don't panic. Don't keep apologising. If it doesn't work after a few minutes, do something different. You are the teacher; you are resourceful! If you stay calm you will be able to think of something else that will be productive for your students. You could review the course/module so far. You could pose some questions or problems which students could discuss in buzz groups (2/3/4 students discussing for between 2 and 5 minutes) and then canvass answers/contributions. You are a professional. You can think on your feet. You can control the situation. Don't let your own disappointment or anger get the better of you. The students will respect your professionalism and your resourcefulness in adversity more than your attacks on inanimate objects (or on the presumed incompetence of support services).

Minimise the chances of it going wrong. Don't use more complicated systems than you need or are familiar with. When you know you will encounter an unfamiliar venue with unfamiliar equipment (and interconnects), don't take risks - so don't use computer presentation when you could use overhead transparencies instead.

If equipment malfunction will seriously upset the course (e.g. cross-links, assignment schedules etc.) then take some time in advance to check everything works as you wish. But still have a back-up plan just in case.

KEY: You are the major resource. You are a professional. You can cope constructively with situations where resources like equipment or software fail to work. You can still work when all else around you malfunctions.

Your Attitude to Your Audience:

Avoid using equipment and gizmos just for the sake of it or to impress your students. They will see through you, and it is likely to have the opposite effect to the one you intend. Your aim should be to communicate, not to show off you or your technology.

Try to avoid giving the impression you have done this 'lecture' many times before, even if you have. Never say things like, "I'm sorry about the quality of these overhead transparencies, I did them at midnight last night/on the train here/five minutes ago." - even if you did. Make your audience feel valued by giving the impression that this is a unique event. Even if most of the resources you are using are not specially prepared for the occasion, try to have something which signals that you have thought about this particular audience as maybe a bit different from any other.

Likewise, avoid the 'corporate' presentation. It suggests that your corporate image is more important to you than your audience. And anyway, slide after slide with the same corporate logo means that each slide blurs into the next, such that any distinctive visual 'hook' each slide may have is undermined. Be subtle: prove yourself to be an effective communicator with something significant to convey, and then associate it with anything external whose profile you may wish to enhance.

KEY: Respect your audience. Direct all your skill with educational media at effective communication, and at their needs as learners.

Activity and Interactivity:

Without doubt effective use of educational media can dramatically improve communication with your students. Unfortunately, good communication will not necessarily maximise student learning. Although students may clearly understand what you are saying, and the flow of your argument, they may not be able to relate this fresh knowledge to prior learning and understanding. To some extent you can help them integrate the new material into their established mental frameworks by the way you present it - drawing connections to previous elements in the course, and giving examples and illustrations that contextualise and, ideally, relate to your students' prior knowledge and experience.

But this is not sufficient because each student's mental 'set' will be slightly different, and you cannot guarantee that your chosen explanations and examples will be enough on their own to enable every student to take personal possession. You can facilitate this 'ownership' (and therefore, real understanding) by engaging the students in activities - asking questions or setting problems that demand active thinking from your audience. One difficulty here is that you cannot usually ask for a response from every student. Students know this and therefore many do not exert themselves, relying on the more forward members of the audience to do all the work.

A more effective way of engaging students is through interactivity - getting students to discuss with each other. There is really no venue where this cannot be achieved in some way, though the layout and seating may influence the length of discussion before students begin to feel uncomfortable; this is likely to be from a few minutes in a lecture theatre, up to half and hour or more seated round a table with easy eye contact between all group members. A spokesperson from the group then gives feedback on its discussion to the whole student body.

You will find many variations on these techniques in the other books in the SEDA Specials series. But just as the use of educational media can transform the effectiveness of communication, so the same media can promote and support activity and interactivity in powerful ways and thus radically improve student learning. Many possibilities are outlined in this book, such as using flipchart paper for students to summarise their discussion, using OHP transparencies cut into pieces to collect student responses, or using a short clip from a video or a newspaper report as a trigger to discussion. The possibilities are endless.

KEY: A part of your thinking and preparation should always be "How can I use educational media to promote and support student activity and interactivity, as well as to improve communication?"

Learning Materials:

So far the discussion has largely covered the use of educational media for lectures, seminars, tutorials and other face-to-face presentations.

Many of the general points about communication and learning apply equally to the use of media to support individual or group study. However, without the teacher present to guide and explain there is a need for much more detailed preparation in terms of instructions, explanations, and generating activity and interactivity. Text-based materials will be enhanced by the addition of images in terms of visual interest and variety, but these can be used in ways much more central to student learning. Slides and videos can be used in learning packs as core materials, supported by written guides to study. There is an unhelpful emphasis on computer-based learning in this area, to the neglect of other, often simpler, methods. You will find a number of suggestions in this book.

KEY: Don't neglect the use of educational media to support individual and group learning. There are simpler ways than computer-based packages

Chapter 3: Blackboards, Whiteboards and Flipcharts

Tradition:

Traditionally, lecturers have used blackboards and chalk (today more often the whiteboard and marker pen) to support the spoken element in lectures and presentations. Hence, the expression 'chalk and talk' which has acquired quite a pejorative meaning implying lack of imagination, tedium, and inflexible didacticism - with some justification. As an undergraduate I went to many lectures where lecturers copied from their notes (often in turn copied from text books) on to the chalkboard, and we students laboriously copied from the board into our notebooks, as though we were still locked into some kind of medieval monasticism and the printing press had never been invented. The lecturer would do this every year with little change, if any. It was (and is, for it still happens) a mockery of any claim for universities to be 'seats of learning' - seats of passivity and boredom would be a better description.

Modern Approaches:

This is not to dismiss the blackboard. It has its uses as a kind of 'jotter' for spontaneous thoughts, recording student feedback or just clarifying awkward spellings. The overhead projector (OHP) has replaced the board as a means of delivering preconceived material in a visual form.

You do not have to turn your back on the audience to use the OHP, so you do not lose 'contact' with them, and your voice does not become muffled and inaudible.

Transparencies can be prepared in advance so that time is not wasted while the lecturer writes in public. This does not exclude the spontaneous: you can add to prepared transparencies as you go along, or you can also use blank transparencies, like the blackboard, as a jotter.

Readability:

Whichever medium you use, make sure your writing is legible. Take some time to practise in the empty venue, walking around the room or lecture theatre, ensuring your writing is readable from every position. And not just readable; remember some students will not have 20/20 vision. Your writing should be well above minimum thresholds of legibility. Printed style letters are generally easier to read than joined up unless you make the latter quite square and upright.

Flipcharts:

These are very useful in smaller rooms, particularly for seminars and tutorials.

A flipchart is a pad of large format paper supported on a stand (Fig.1). Sheets can be simply torn off, or folded over the back of the stand so that they can easily be flipped back to the front when required for discussion again.

One major advantage is that you can bring your writing close to the students, or wherever it is required in the room. You are not restricted by the fixed position of a blackboard or whiteboard.

Another advantage is that there is no need to erase when space runs out. Simply flip to a new sheet. Nothing is lost and you can quickly recover material from earlier in the session. As with the OHP, you can prepare visual material well in advance.

Flipcharts and Interactivity:

However, flipcharts really come into their own when you have interactive sessions with groups of students engaged in peer discussion or activity. Each group can prepare feedback on flipchart sheets for presentation in a plenary.

Another use is for 'poster' sessions. Each group's work is pinned or stuck on the walls of the room while students move from poster to poster reading the outcomes of other groups or individuals.

I personally like to have a flip chart to hand when working in seminar or tutorial mode - just in case the need arises to summarise or review in a written format. The greater 'intimacy' of the flipchart somehow increases students readiness to respond - perhaps because you don't have to walk away or turn your back on them. It is much easier to retain eye contact.

A big spin-off is that you the lecturer can collect all the sheets and posters after a seminar, compile the feedback, and present it back to your students in a structured form, typed-up and photocopied.

KEY: Don't waste time copying to a board. Use the OHP or flipchart to preprepare written notes, cues and diagrams. Check that your writing is large enough and legible, whatever the medium.

Figure 1: A Flipchart and Stand

Group of students
prepares feedback
on flipchart sheet

Students read sheets
pinned to wall: posters

Student presents
group feedback in
plenary session

Teacher using flipchart
for small groupwork
e.g. seminar

Figure 2: Ideal Overhead Projector Set-up

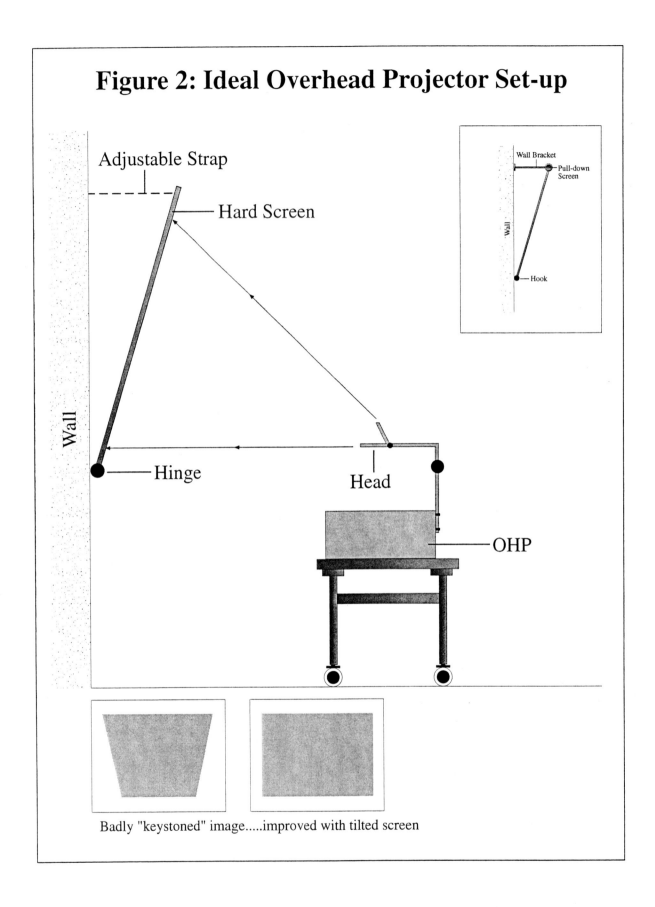

Badly "keystoned" image.....improved with tilted screen

Chapter 4: The Overhead Projector (OHP)

Learn to use this tool well and you will have learned a lot about the power of educational media to improve communication - and about integrating the visual with the verbal.

Advantages:

The OHP is designed for use in relatively high ambient light conditions. It should not be necessary to dim the normal lighting or use blackout, though sometimes effectiveness can be improved by angling the screen away from windows or lights, or closing a few blinds and switching off part of the lighting in particularly bright conditions.

Projectors of different powers suit different settings. Large or particularly sunny venues need 400 watt projectors, or larger. The very high powered OHPs do not switch to full brightness immediately, which can be disconcerting. They slowly get brighter over several minutes. This is designed to extend lamp life.

The basic idea of the OHP is that normal lighting conditions can be maintained so that students can see to take notes (unlike slides), and the lecturer does not have to turn his or her back to the audience (as with the chalkboard). In other words, the OHP maximises communication and note-taking possibilities. The lecturer retains eye contact, and students can see the lecturer's lips move - and it is not only hearing impaired students who benefit from this.

You can prepare your transparencies in advance, and add to them as your lecture proceeds if necessary. You don't have to waste time copying to a chalkboard or whiteboard.

Setting Up the OHP:

The overhead projector is thus named because it can project upwards at an angle so that the image can be seen without obstruction by all members of the audience.

This means keeping the projector fairly low down so that its head is not in anyone's line of vision, and the mirror is tilted to project the image upwards as far as the screen will allow. Projecting upwards to a vertical screen causes 'keystoning' where the sides of the image converge downwards. Good projection screens can be tilted downwards (or the bottom pinned back) (Fig.2) to correct this effect. Having done this, move the projector back until the image fills the whole screen - though beware that the lower part of the screen is not visible to some of the audience, in which case rather than go for a smaller image it may be better to move the transparency up the screen as you go through it.

Keystoning can sometimes be so severe that the lettering at the bottom is illegibly small: it can seem like an optician's test card. Unfortunately, many screens cannot be tilted, and the stand for the OHP is too high. I sometimes move the OHP to a chair and tilt it upwards a bit in such situations. Even if you cannot get rid of keystoning you can try to get the OHP head out of the line of vision of members of your audience.

Figure 3: Overhead Projector Controls

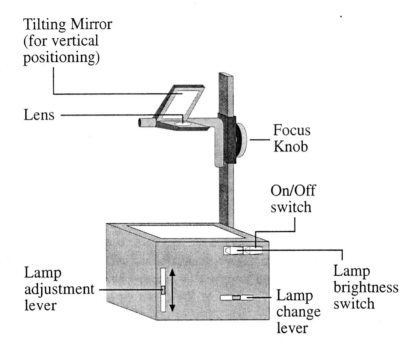

Tilting Mirror
(for vertical
positioning)

Lens

Focus
Knob

On/Off
switch

Lamp
adjustment
lever

Lamp
change
lever

Lamp
brightness
switch

*Position and character of controls varies between makes

The Controls:

OHPs vary in the configuration and type of control, with a mixture of switches, levers, and knobs (Fig. 3).

After switching on, first check that the lamp is correctly positioned internally by checking the image projected without a transparency. This should be as white as possible without coloured blue or pink fringes at the edges. Move the lever or turn the knob on the front of the projector until the image is as uncoloured as you can get it. If the blue, pink or dark casts persist at the edges, report it for servicing.

Now put on a transparency and check focus. If you have difficulty in focusing, check that the head is parallel to the base and that both lens and mirror are clear of dust and fingerprints.

There is often a second lever or switch which changes the bulb. It is surprising how many times distressed lecturers are unaware of this emergency arrangement. However, if you do have to switch to the spare, remember to report that a bulb has blown - otherwise the next time it goes the unfortunate lecturer will switch from one dud to another.

Readability:

Don't overload the transparency (OHT) with information. If necessary spread it across two or more OHTs. Make sure you use large enough lettering to be read at the back of the room. Figure 4 shows the very minimum size of lettering you can get away with in a large room. For a large lecture theatre you will probably need even bigger print, depending on the power of the projector and maximum screen size.

Nicely presented handwritten OHTs are fine, but printed ones can have more impact. Don't use photocopies from books - it will be unreadable a few yards away. If you want to go through extended text, give it as a printed handout.

Don't just put your lecture notes on your OHTs, try to pare down what you include to key words and phrases - this will then act as a cue for you and an aide memoire for students. Figure 4 is a good example of such paring down.

Effective Uses:

- Lay out the structure of your lecture in key words and phrases on an OHT. You can keep referring to it as your talk proceeds.

- Summarise the key points at the end of your lecture on an OHT. You can use it at the beginning of the next lecture as well. Not only will it reinforce student learning, but it will also help to get students' minds in gear before you start on new material.

- For each section of your session (as given in the structure) have an OHT with the key points (not whole sentences - try to get each point into 3 or 4 words or less).

Figure 4: Sample OHT

PRINCIPLES FOR USE OF VIDEO

a) Brevity - i.e. focused

b) Activity
i) before
ii) during
iii) after

c) Interactivity
i) before
ii) during
iii) after

- Use diagrams. This is easy because they can be prepared in advance by hand, photocopied onto acetate from a book, or produced by your Media Services graphics unit (who may be able to prepare nice text-based OHTs as well).

- Use colour and shape. These can make slides more memorable, helping student recall. Both colour and shape (e.g. the way text is laid out, which could be circular, vertical, horizontal, in linked boxes, zig-zag etc.) can be used to track different themes and provide emphasis. Patterns can be really useful to students in structuring their knowledge.

- Use textual variety. Size and type of lettering is good for emphasising hierarchy or equivalence of key points.

- Use reveals. Cover up the OHT and reveal sections in sequence. Use this technique sparingly: your students will probably understand and remember much better if they get an overview of the whole slide before you go through in detail - they will then know better how to locate and relate the detail. Nevertheless, reveals can be used for dramatic effect - a final surprise conclusion for example. They can also be used to make students think ahead through a deductive argument. But don't use them in a 'guess what teacher has written next' mode! If what comes next is not logically deduced but open to debate or choice, then build up an OHT through discussion as you go along.

- Ways of revealing. The simplest way is to use a sheet of paper - put a pen or other object on it to prevent it falling off, or fold the top edge on itself a few times. Non-linear reveals can be achieved by cutting out pieces of card or POST-ITs and placing them over areas in advance, then removing in the chosen sequence - good for diagrams and pictures.

- Use a mask. Projection can be dramatically improved by blanking off the area on the OHP not covered by acetate. You can buy special pouches with opaque wings or just use a piece of card with an A4 hole cut in it. You will be surprised how much more professional your slides will look.

- Overlays. Text or a diagrams can be built up by placing successive transparencies on top of each other. It is a more complex way of slowly revealing the whole picture, but particularly useful where each addition interacts with previous elements in the diagram.

- Use photographs or pictures. A colour photocopier can convert a picture in a book, or a photographic print to an A4 colour transparency. Some copies can convert 35mm slides, and more surprisingly, colour negatives. Be sure to use the correct acetate for photocopiers - acetate for handwritten OHTs will cause serious damage.

- Animation. You can move elements around on the OHP. Cardboard cut outs will give a silhouette effect (e.g. you could move cars and bicycles as silhouettes on an OHT of a road junction to illustrate road safety). Cut out coloured acetate brings more variety to this technique. Engineers have used sophisticated perspex moving models to illustrate mechanical functions (eg. the internal combustion engine).

- Interaction. At the simplest level, question and answer can be used by the lecturer to build up a 'picture' on an OHT. Student responses and views can be included even where an OHT is preprepared - use a permanent pen, or printing, for the initial OHT and add their comments with an erasable pen so you can re-use the original. Even better, blank transparency can be given to students, with pens. In a large lecture you can use cut up A4 acetate to get student responses to a question - several of these can be gathered at one time on the OHT, where a big advantage is that the responses are to all intents and purposes anonymous, making students more confident in responding (don't forget to collect the pens back). In seminars and other group sessions, each group can feed back its discussion via a single transparency, with chosen spokespersons talking the class through each one in turn.

There are many other possibilities - and your imagination is really the limiting factor. The OHP is probably the most versatile tool for face-to-face communication in education. It is readily accessible in most teaching rooms. Even more importantly the teacher has substantial autonomy in its use and in creating 'software' to use on it. That is probably why it is the most ubiquitous piece of educational technology in higher education.

KEY: The overhead projector is such a simple but versatile tool, you will probably learn more about creating and using visual resources to help communicate and structure learning than with any other medium.

Chapter 5: The Rostrum Projector (or Video Visualiser)

This can be used like an OHP. It has both advantages and disadvantages.

The rostrum projector can be bought as a portable item, or it can be built into a venue. Essentially it is made up of a remote control video camera suspended over a flat surface (the document area) which has both overhead lighting (for opaque documents) and lighting from below (for transparencies). The lecturer can zoom in and out and focus using simple controls. (Fig .5)

The venue must have a video projector to a main screen - this is how the audience sees what is being presented under the camera. Substantial enlargement is possible when compared to an OHP, and even standard 12 point text from a book can sometimes be easily read in a lecture theatre. The good depth of field also means that solid objects can be viewed.

A major disadvantage over the OHP is that the house lights will need dimming if the screen image is to be bright enough, increasing the risk of eye strain and loss of concentration for the audience if used for extended periods. But they are becoming more popular because they avoid the need to create transparencies.

If you are attracted to their versatility over the OHP, avoid overuse and giving the whole presentation in a dimly illuminated environment. Switch it off from time to time when not required. The rostrum projector can be connected to the house lights so that the latter automatically dims and rises as the projector is switched on and off.

Rostrum projectors are particularly useful for antiquarian and other fragile material. Most alternative systems require very bright lights either for copying or projection, which can cause irreversible damage.

KEY: A video rostrum projector is particularly good for projecting pages from books (especially antiquarian) and for greatly enlarged images or three dimensional objects.

Figure 5: Rostrum Projector

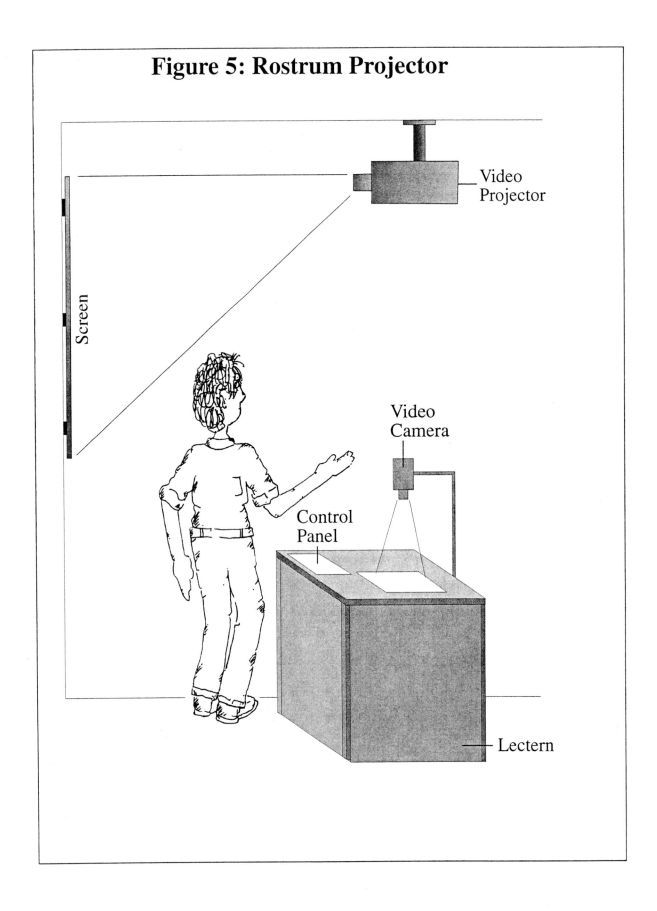

Chapter 6: Slides

Still Images:

Research has indicated that still images can be just as effective as moving images unless continuous movement is itself crucial to understanding. In fact, slides can usefully 'suspend' movement to improve understanding of the process, particularly in this age of motorised cameras which can capture one or more images a second. (For information, film and video use 25 images a second). The first scientific analyses of humans and horses running used numerous still images from a series of running 'events' to piece together the movement of limbs and muscles.

Today it is relatively easy for anyone including children to take good quality photographs -prints or slides. The study of the arts, sciences, engineering, would be severely hampered without access to such good quality images. In most universities and colleges you can borrow a camera and film to take your own shots on location (such as field trips), or request slides copied from books or other material (subject to copyright restrictions).

Slides can offer very high quality images - with good definition and colour saturation (density). However, a disadvantage is that the house lights need to be low to take full advantage of these benefits.

Text based slides can also be used rather than OHTs. This is particularly advantageous if you want to alternate images with text, but necessarily lowered lights makes it less attractive for text only.

The projector:

Slide projection systems are quite sophisticated these days, though simple to operate. The remote control usually offers slide forwards/backwards and focus.

For really slick presentations two linked projectors can be used to 'dissolve' from one slide to another rather than 'flick' between them.

Most projectors use some form of cassette system, the most popular being the circular carousel. Make sure you fully understand how to load the carousel (or cassette) on to the projector. Usually it will only go on or come off when located to the 'zero' position. A release button on the body of the projector will allow you to turn the carousel by hand so that its 'O' point is over the projection gate, for removal. Practise this several times. Don't leave a slide in the projector.

Preparing Your Slides:

Slot your slides in order into the cassette. There is a right way and a wrong way to do this because the projector lens inverts the image. Slides should be upside down and the left side of the picture should be on the right hand side as you drop the slide into its slot, seen from the rear of the projector.

Put slides in sequences. If you intend one slide to follow another without breaks, put them in adjacent slots.

If you intend to stop between slides, leave a blank slot - modern projectors 'shut down' when the gate is empty, so nothing is projected, and the screen is dark rather than illuminated. You can raise the house lights without the distraction of something on the screen.

Computer-generated slides:

The equipment to produce slides of the image on a computer screen is relatively expensive, and you may find your institution makes a not insubstantial charge. So it can be a rather expensive way of turning a computer-based presentation (such as generated by Powerpoint) into a slide presentation. But as a facility for bringing computer screens into the classroom or lecture-theatre without the complexity of setting up a computer projection system, it is invaluable. It is equally invaluable for getting a high quality copy of a computer graphic -generally higher quality than a colour printer will provide.

Ask your computer services or media services department for advice on how to save your computer material for conversion to a slide.

Tape/Slide Programmes:

Once trumpeted as the medium for audiovisual learning packages, the combination of a slide show with a commentary recorded on tape has been largely superseded by the convenience of the videocassette. Tape/slide has always been an awkward medium to set up well, even when automated using audible or inaudible cues on the tape to operate the projector at the right time. There are still some champions of the method because of the ease with which slides and sound track can be made by the relative amateur. Today, domestic video equipment, such as camcorders, can offer similar autonomy to the teacher. (See Chapter 8: Creating and Customising Video).

Slides on Tape:

An effective way of avoiding the problems associated with slide projectors and carousels is to put your slide show on videotape. Many universities have media services departments with telecine benches which can transfer still photos and film to videotape. It is then easy to add a spoken commentary, producing a tape/slide show on videotape. Whether silent or with soundtrack, slides on tape are a convenient medium for students to use for study in private, in a learning centre, or even at home (particularly for part-time students). If your Media Services can produce a master tape in a professional format, as many VHS copies as you want can be made.

A disadvantage is that the duration of each slide has to be fixed in advance. Of course, you or the students can use the freeze-frame facility on the playback VCR. This will be fine with a good quality VCR. Ignore any know-all who tells you this will cause excessive tape wear. By the time it does the content will be out-of-date anyway!

KEY: Even the relative amateur can use a 35mm camera to create slides to support teaching and learning. Don't just verbalise, visualise!

Chapter 7: Using Video

Video is not as popular as a teaching and learning medium as it deserves to be and there are several reasons for this.

a. Difficulty of creating customised programmes;
b. Access to playback systems;
c. Copyright and recording problems;
d. Ignorance about how to use it effectively.

Creating Your Own Programmes:

This is not as difficult as you may think, and I deal with it in the next chapter.

Access to Playback Systems:

The ready availability of VHS videocassette recorders (VCR) and the cheapness of tapes should mean that most institutions can afford to provide ready access. Lecture theatres usually have playback to the main screen built in, and other rooms may have permanent systems or portable systems on a trolley close by. Students can gain access in libraries and learning centres, and at home (of particular significance for part-time students). Unfortunately there is even less standardisation of controls than on OHPs, and modern machines have the annoying habit of starting to play on insertion of the tape. But a couple of minutes examination should enable you to take charge of play, stop, fastforward, rewind and eject (often the same button as 'stop'). Note as well that on some TVs a red light indicates 'standby' and you must press the 'on' button to get a green light before a picture will appear. The TV must also be set to the correct channel for the VCR.

Copyright and Recording:

The 1988 Copyright Act imposed an obligation on TV broadcasters to license educational use of programmes recorded 'off-air'. In the absence of such a licence, programmes could be freely used in education in the UK (assuming there was no commercial gain from such use). The terrestrial TV stations (BBC and commercial) joined together to form ERA, the Educational Recording Agency. The annual licence is based on a flat charge per FTE student (currently around £1.50) and not on the number of programmes held. The Open University (OU) has its own licensing arrangement, based on the number of programmes held (around £12 per programme per year).

The ERA licence licenses any employee or student in the institution to make recordings, and copy them if required, for educational purposes **in that institution.** The OU licence only licenses a nominated licensee (usually in the institution's video unit) to make recordings - no one else can legally record them. For this reason and others (mainly convenience and cataloguing) most institutions have an off-air recording service. The University of Derby has around 4,000 programmes available, listed by title and subject in an on-line catalogue. A big advantage of using the central service is that tapes are stored centrally (and catalogued) rather than lost on the shelves of individuals. If stored in a library or learning centre, students can gain access - very important as we move more towards student-centredness, resource-based learning, and independent study.

Using Video Effectively:

There is a mistaken belief that has grown up around the use of TV in education over the last 30 years: that because students are used to high quality domestic TV, in education we must replicate broadcast standards.

This is mistaken in two ways:

- Students do not demand that printed handouts replicate the high quality print, graphics and photography of magazines they read in their leisure time. On the contrary, they value highly the simple customised, low printed quality handouts their lecturers give them because they expect such resources to be highly relevant and fit for the purpose of learning. Why should video be any different, so long as the quality is fit-for-purpose?

- The last thing we should try to replicate is the aura of domestic TV in the domestic lounge. It spells passivity, intellectual shallowness, entertainment, intermittent attention. On the contrary, we need to make video in education active, intellectually challenging, serious and relevant.

Not surprisingly, because of this mistaken belief, video in HE is used too often in shallow ways - to entertain, to provide relaxation, to let the teacher get on with something else while keeping the students happy! So here are some basic tips to using video in teaching:

- Avoid passivity. Use video in short bursts (i.e. just a few minutes).

- Engage the students, before, during and after. Get their minds on track by posing questions, perhaps with discussion, before showing the clip. Give them something to do or think about while watching. Get them into discussion amongst themselves afterwards.

- Make sure your choice of video is focused, and not firing off in all directions - another reason for using clips rather than whole programmes. You will find that by taking a few short sequences you will actually cover more ground more deeply than by showing a whole video and then asking, "What did you think of that?"

As you become more confident in the practical aspects of using video, you may wish to use it in more sophisticated ways. Here are a few suggestions:

- Where the video is the 'film of the book', engage students in close analysis and comparison - this can be done with extracts.

- For a documentary, examine the 'point of view' of the makers. This is good for developing critical skills, and can be easier to set up in class than textual analysis.

- Suggest the students 'rework' the programme, or extract i.e. draw up their own 'storyboard'. Good for groupwork, or project work. Good for developing visualisation skills in your students.

Preparing to Use Video:

* You will need to cue-up your tape to your selected start point, allowing a few seconds before it for the VCR to get going.

* You don't want to waste too much time fastforwarding to another point. Give the students something to do while you find your next section. Or get your extracts copied to another tape - limited editing/ extraction is legal under the ERA licence, provided you do not alter the producers' intentions (eg make it say the opposite). But speak to the licence holder in your institution first.

* Ensure playback facilities are adequate. A 28" TV monitor may not be adequate in a large room, and you may need to order a projector and screen.

KEY: Use video with brevity, focus and activity.

Figure 6: Basic VESOL System

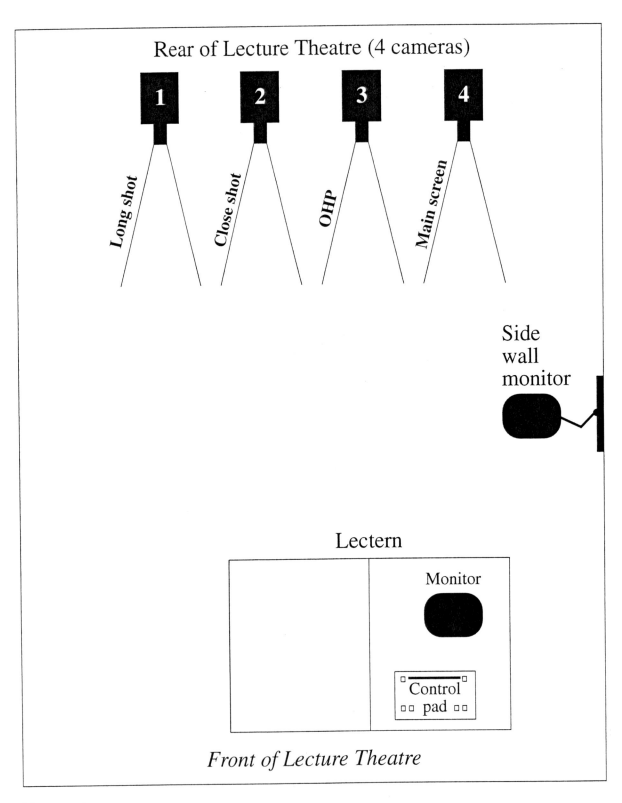

Not to scale

Chapter 8: Creating and Customising Video

Studio production is not the only way to produce educational videos. Nor do you necessarily need expensive equipment. 'Domestic' equipment has improved dramatically in recent years, in both quality and ease of use.

Studio Production:

This is expensive and time-consuming and requires a lot of technical support. Most lecturers balk at the prospect, but if your institution has facilities, then talk to the video producer about your ideas for video in teaching and learning. There are occasions where high quality production is desirable - if there is commercial potential, for example.

Using Mainly Stills:

This was discussed in the chapter on Slides. The idea can be expanded to include simple graphics and text screens alongside your pictures. This is relatively cheap, and has much simpler production and editing requirements. Most importantly, you the teacher have much more control over the process.

It is a good way to produce a video for independent learning, tutorless groups, or distance learning - you can include on-screen instructions. In general, editing captions giving instructions to the viewer(s) onto any video is possible. It is also easy to add a spoken commentary.

Using 'Found' Video Materials:

Customising off-air video and commercial educational videos encounters copyright difficulties. Limited editing is possible under the ERA licence e.g. pulling out a few extracts to promote student discussion. Using a camcorder you can of course generate your own material which can be simply edited, with graphics and captions if required.

Video Production Systems:

These are systems for recording lectures and other teaching activities. Mostly, they require technical support in attendance, which can complicate production - you, the teacher will have to explain to the technicians what you are going to do, and in turn they will set limitations on where you can stand and what you can do.

However, at the University of Derby we have invented a family of systems requiring no technical support. You, the teacher, are in complete control. The basic system is VESOL -Video autoproduction and Editing System for Open Learning (Fig. 6) - which empowers lecturers to record their presentations in front of a live audience in real time. In other words, a video can be produced during normal teaching with little extra effort. On first hearing of this, academics are generally highly sceptical. But when they see the system and have some hands-on experience, they are astonished at how simple it is. We have had a 64 year-old lecturer produce programmes after just a few minutes practice. The quality of the presentation is more important than the technical quality, provided the latter is fit-for-purpose.

Systems have been developed for workshops and laboratories, VELAB. MiniVESOL (Fig. 7) is a system in a small room where lecturers can build up programmes in comfort and in private. MiniVESOL has been connected to a Videophone so that even videoconferencing can be recorded. Systems will accommodate all the usual presentation methods (whiteboard, slides, video, OHP, rostrum projection, computer output). A big advantage over studio-based production, apart from simplicity and cost, is that the lecturer is in her or his familiar environment rather than having to adapt to a studio.

VESOL-based systems are now being used in other institutions, and the key ideas of simplicity and autonomous production have been widely adapted, e.g. as the front end of a system sending lectures live to a distant site. See Further Help for access to more information about VESOL.

KEY: Keep your custom videos relatively simple. Little can be added educationally, and a lot can be subtracted, by adopting unnecessarily high production values.

Figure 7: MiniVESOL with Videophone

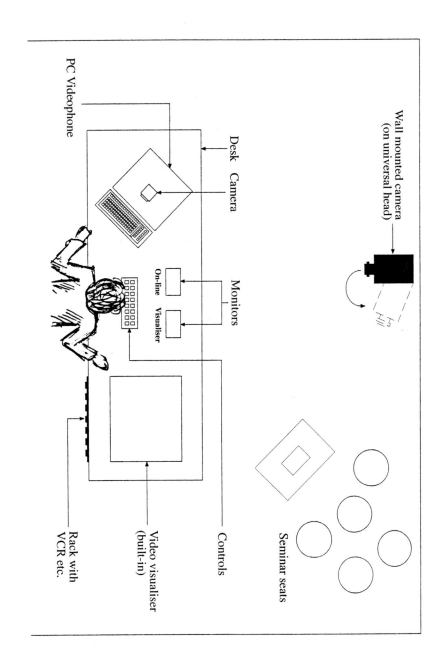

Figure 8

Science and Society
Plan and Structure for Note Taking
Lecture IX

The Nature of Scientific Method

Reading   A F Chalmers: What is this thing called science?
                             Open U.P, 1978. Chaps 1, 2 and 3

            M Mulkay: Science and the Sociology of Knowledge
                             George Allen and Unwin, 1979 Chaps 1 & 2

            K Popper: Conjectures and Refutations RKP 1963

1   Introduction

Can the validity, the truth of scientific theories be demonstrated? Is scientific discovery a strictly logical process - is it even rational? How do theories arise and how are they developed, changed and replaced? How do scientists think - and do they operate as they should in order to claim to be "scientific"?

These are some of the important questions I will address in the next three weeks.

2   Deduction and Induction

    A   From the general to the particular - deduction

    B   From the particular to the general - induction

    C Problems: What 'facts' do you look for? Are facts factual?

3   The Hypothetico-Deductive Method

    A   Start from theory, not facts.

B   Hypothesis not arrived at logically - but imaginatively, intuitively, poetically etc - eg Kekule, Watson and Crick.

C   Hypothesis makes predictions, by deduction, which are tested experimentally .

D   If results support original deductions, then the hypothesis is deemed <u>confirmed.</u>

<u>4</u>   <u>Popper's Conjectures and Refutations</u>

A   Falsification not confirmation: scientists should seek to refute their imaginative <u>conjectures.</u> Trying to <u>confirm</u> them is not scientific. The logic of scientific discovery is <u>falsification!</u>

B   Falsification and the demarcation of science: a true scientific theory must be <u>in principle</u> falsifiable. "The moon is made of green cheese" is a scientific theory "God is good" is not scientific, it is a metaphysical theory.

C   Freudianism Marxism and Darwinism are all metaphysical and cannot claim to be scientific.

D   Poppers theory of falsification falsified - or at least questioned

5   Instrumentalism and Realism

A   Why this concern over the scientific method? Surely the fact that a theory is <u>useful,</u> that it <u>works</u> is enough - the instrumentalist view.

B   But who is satisfied with this? We all want to be <u>right</u>, and so many scientists and many philosophers, like Popper, want to believe each theoretical 'advance' gets closer to a description of 'reality' - the realist view.

C   A realist needs to prove his/her theory is a true description, or as close to it as is currently possible.

D   Since the beginning of the seventeenth century, when Galileo set the cat among the Inquisitional pigeons by claiming that heliocentrism was a true and not just a useful theory, - there have been attempts to show that scientific method is as logical as mathematical proof. As we have seen, none of the attempts really stands up so far.

Conclusions

A   Scientific method does not follow a clear logic.
B   There is a strong element of imagination.
C   Theory comes before the facts which eventually may support it.
D   Observational 'facts' may rejected in favour of theory.
E   Theories cannot be convincingly confirmed or even falsified. So what is the status of a theory which is obviously useful? Can we only claim it as a man-made instrument and not a 'truth' of Nature?

13/11/90
CMO'H/HB

Chapter 9: Handouts and Booklets

These are the staple of customised resources for supporting both teaching and learning in HE. The photocopier has revolutionised the ease with which materials can be copied, and the wordprocessor has revolutionised the ease with which teachers can themselves generate nicely presented printed materials. And the existence of the CLA, The Copyright Licensing Agency, has enabled institutions to buy licences to make multiple copies of extracts from books and periodicals.

Power of Handouts:

Students value more than anything else (rightly or wrongly!) the customised printed resources they are given by their teachers. Why? Because they assume (rightly) that these resources relate most closely to the teacher's expectations of them, and will therefore pay off in their assignments and exams. Given such expectations, the preparation of these materials merits considerable thought.

Ideas for Handouts:

- Rather than give out full lecture notes, or none at all, prepare skeleton notes which have the essentials in terms of structure, key points and diagrams. Leave space in each section for students to add the detail and examples (Fig. 8). You will know that their note-taking is consequently correctly focused. They are also likely to remain more alert, neither losing attention nor writing everything down indiscriminately (listening to everything but hearing nothing). Students can use the blank spaces to write in the detail they need to clarify the key points, plus examples etc. The emphasis is on understanding not recording. Don't forget to think of activities. For example at 4B students could be asked to think up some falsifiable and unfalsifiable hypotheses.

- Prepare written instructions for assignments and project work, indicating how marks will be distributed. Give examples of essay structures, project headings, solving problems, and the marking balance. Students often fail to perform because they don't understand the parameters of assessment.

- Prepare a set of illustrative 'mini-scenarios' or problems for students to discuss at appropriate points in your course. Giving them out in advance may stimulate thought and help students better understand the context of their learning.

- Don't hand out printed copies of your OHTs before the lecture unless you are confident it will help rather than distract. You can tell students they will get a copy at the end, and then you will have their full attention undistracted by copying.

- You can paste photos and diagrams into your handouts . Today's photocopiers cope extremely well. Figure 8 has a course 'logo' pasted on, which helps students identify materials but can also help create an identity for the course team.

Booklets:

These can support individual and group study.

- Prepare a booklet to support a coming seminar - it may include a journal article or two.

- Turn a lecture into a booklet and give it out the week before, for discussion the following week.

- Include small assignments and tests to keep students active.

KEY: Students value handouts because they see them as key guides to what they are expected to learn, and to how they are assessed. Handouts become a personal possession, so provide this guidance clearly and unambiguously in this easily filed and digested format.

Chapter 10: Using Computers

I think the computer is a wonderful tool. Computers are opening up new possibilities for teachers and learners. However, supporters can be obsessive about them to the point of seriously overplaying their strengths and undervaluing the strengths of other media. So I would like to briefly examine some of the excessive claims made by these obsessives - to help you should you encounter one of them.

Digital Versus Analogue:

We are generally moving towards more and more use of digital technology - but this does not mean we have to reject tried and tested 'old' technologies. Much of the latter will eventually be replaced by digital processes, but it will be gradual. At first, digital replacements are often more expensive and do not live up to the grandiose claims made by the manufacturers and suppliers. So there is a lot to be said for sticking to the familiar, if it is fit-for-purpose, and waiting for the new technology to become relatively cheap, reliable, and easy to use. There is an enormous investment worldwide in analogue television and video systems, for example, so it will be a long time before current equipment is completely outmoded. This book will be out-of-date before then.

Analogue and digital systems can coexist, with analogue-to-digital and digital-to-analogue transfer as necessary. Let us not forget that we see and hear in analogue modes, so we will never escape the need for such transfers.

Interactivity:

The term 'interactive' has been rudely hijacked by supporters of computer-assisted learning -almost with relief, because of the general failure of programmed learning systems in the past. The lack of 'interactivity', or inability to respond to different learner needs and pathways, is often given as the main reason for that failure.

But what kind of interactivity will help our students to learn? Ultimately, it is the interactivity in their minds, in the dialogue that goes on between what-I-already-know-and-understand and what-I-am-trying-to-learn-and-understand. We need to promote that internal dialogue, and there are many ways of doing it. Computer-assisted learning may be one of them - at its best, a very effective method. But the dialogue with the teacher, with fellow students, with the author of a book as the student interrogates what he or she is reading, are all good methods as well, and at their best, highly effective.

Linearity:

The 'non-linearity' of computer-based packages is often promoted as superior to supposed linear systems like videotape, or books. But everything is linear in time, even computer-assisted learning. And it is simply false that books etc. are structurally linear. Arguments proposed in books or on film are often multi-branching, and anyone writing a structurally linear novel or film script today will have difficulty in finding a publisher or producer - the flash-back/forward and sub-plot are as much staples of fiction as multibranching is of serious non-fiction.

In fact it has been argued that the 'continuity' of books and films offers students clear and more varied models and exemplars for the construction of knowledge and understanding, where cyber-space and hyperlinked systems tend to the amorphous and confusing. This is supported by evidence that basic familiarity with a subject is required before students can benefit from the freedom to explore what hyperlinking offers.

Flexibility:

To be sure, multimedia computers offer the remarkable flexibility to use a variety of audio-visual media within a single box, and to access an extraordinary variety of resources worldwide. But you can't read it in the bath, and portable systems are generally expensive and limited. Most people in the developed world have access to a television and a videorecorder at home. Only a small minority have computers, and even fewer have on-line services. This will change, and the computer will grow in relevance and flexibility. As teachers we will need to grow with that development. We will not be helped in that growth by an obsessive concentration on computer-based methods. In fact, because the computer is a multimedia medium, learning to use these separate media in precise ways for communication and learning can only help us to use multimedia computers more effectively in the long term.

Computers in Teaching:

At the simplest level, there is often a need to show students what computers can do. This is best done hands-on in a computer suite, but a demonstration and explanation in class can help prepare for this. A large monitor may suffice, but some form of projection to a screen may be necessary.

There are two main methods of projecting computer output:

- the lcd (liquid crystal display) tablet placed on an OHP. This needs a powerful OHP, preferably more powerful than 400 watts.

- the lcd projector. These are now much smaller and easier to use.

However both systems will usually require that the lights are lowered. I have noticed that extended computer presentations cause eye-strain and loss of concentration, so it is a good idea to raise the lights from time to time. They are also quite noisy, from the fans used to cool the electronics - the relief from those nearby when the equipment is turned off can be tangible!

It has become common for presenters to use computer presentation, not to illustrate what a computer does, but as a replacement for the OHP, using slide-generating software (like Powerpoint) to produce the equivalent of a series of OHTs. I would urge you to think carefully first, because we are still some way away from being able to do this in normal ambient lighting conditions, and so it is inevitable that effective communication, audience concentration, and ability to take notes easily will be adversely affected. If you do decide to use computer-based presentations, plan your slides as carefully as you would for OHP transparencies, use 'reveals' sparingly, avoid difficult to read colour combinations, use large lettering, and raise the house lights regularly.

KEY: When using computer projection for presentations keep the periods the audience is required to watch the screen relatively short, to avoid eyestrain and loss of attention.

Chapter 11: Computers Supporting Learning

I do not intend here to go into the growing number of computer packages available to support independent study - such as the resources generated by schemes like TLTP (Teaching and Learning Technology Programme). I suggest you contact a relevant CTI (Computers in Teaching Initiative) Centre or a TLTSN (Teaching and Learning Technology Support Network) Centre for free assistance. See the chapter Further Help.

Computers for Communication:

This is one of the great strengths of computer technology. At the simplest level, email (electronic mail) is very convenient, and allows students to ask questions of their teachers without making an appointment, and allows teachers the time to make a considered reply.

Email Conferencing systems bring some structure to this, and allow all your students to read the same questions and answers. Conferences can have different threads and these can easily be separated into different conferences rather than muddled together. A major difficulty can be getting students to participate in these on-line, asynchronous discussions. The most successful solution is to make on-line participation an assessed course requirement, though how you assess is less clear. A simple method is to treat it like an attendance requirement -below a certain level of participation the student is considered to have failed the course.

Videoconferencing is gaining in popularity, and there are now many systems for achieving this form of face-to-face discussion at a distance. It is more expensive and demanding than email conferencing. It is of course synchronous rather than asynchronous like email, and there are some who believe that asynchronicity is superior because it allows for more deliberation and assimilation, and more opportunity for sharing the discussion with others. It also has the advantage of restoring the written word to a significance that has been lost since the telephone (synchronous) eroded the use of the letter (asynchronous).

As teachers we can learn a tremendous amount from fellow teachers. Joining one or two email discussion lists in your subject area or in other interests is essential to your growth as an effective teacher and/or researcher. See Chapter 13, Further Help, for information about Mailbase.

Talk to your Computing Services and/or Media Services about software and systems for both synchronous and asynchronous conferencing.

Authoring for Computers:

There are two main ways: the multimedia tutorial stored on floppy disk, hard disk or CDROM; and learning material authored on WWW pages. The distinction is beginning to blur as multimedia packages include connections to the WWW, and the WWW itself is beginning to be used to deliver multimedia tutorials.

To produce a tutorial you need to use authoring software. This is usually quite complex to master and best left to professional authors - your institution will probably have a multimedia authoring facility. However, less complex 'shells' can be created from authoring software, which provide templates for the simple insertion of learning materials, such as text, graphics, video, assessments, etc. At the University of Derby we have developed TOTAL (Tutor Only Transfer of Authored Learning - see Further Help) but it is often better to specify your own template for tutorials and ask someone to produce a customised shell for you.

It is now relatively easy to put material onto the WWW - there is no need to learn HTML, Hypertext Markup Language (though it is not at all difficult) because modern wordprocessors can convert text files into HTML. You may need some help in converting graphics and other images into a WWW format. But overall, it is a lot easier than it may seem.

There is an awful lot of dross around in the form of multimedia and WWW sites. Mastery of the technical issues is not sufficient to guarantee worthwhile resources. Using computers to support student learning is more demanding on teachers than using most other educational media. I would urge you to develop your skills with all the other media described in this booklet - learning to combine text, images and sound in your teaching and in the materials you create for your students for independent study. You will find you have developed a bank of resources which are tried and tested, which can then be readily converted to computer delivery.

An additional complexity is Copyright. There are currently no licensing schemes which permit the conversion of printed, photographic, or video material to digital format for delivery in multimedia or over the WWW. Express permission from copyright holders must be sought. You should also remember that all materials on the WWW are copyright and that it is strictly speaking not legal to print, or copy electronically. It would be a major breach of copyright to use such copied materials in your teaching without permission. You can of course refer students, or provide hot links, to specific WWW sites. However, copyright holders are very often pleased to grant limited permissions for use in non-profit making educational activity. Try asking, but make it clear how you intend to use the material.

KEY: Learn to use the computer for communications - word processing and email - first. Set up email conferences for your students. Find out about software in your subject area, use what is good, and then, and only then, consider creating resources yourself.

Chapter 12: Media in Extended Student Activity

We live in a society increasingly dominated by audiovisual media. We owe it to our students to develop an understanding of the communications power of these media, and develop the skills to critically analyse how they are manipulated. Most students do not have Media Studies modules in their courses where such matters are explicitly explored, but we can allow such exploration and discussion through project work, without losing sight of normal course requirements.

Mixed Media Stands:

Students (individually or as a small team) are required to put together a stand - usually a small table with a display panel or wall behind it. Text, posters, photographs, audio tape, video, solid objects can all be used subject to the availability of facilities. The display must have more than just a theme supporting a motley collection of material - it must have a thesis, a message to which all the resources contribute. It is a good idea if the students are required to articulate the thesis in a single sentence.

The advantage of such displays is that all the students on the course can spend an afternoon looking at their peers' work. You can even use peer assessment, which has its merits for this kind of project work where the teacher may be accused of too much subjective judgement. Have a marking pro forma (Fig 9). Average the student marks out of 50, and give your own mark out of 50 to obtain a final percentage result. I usually say I will exclude the top two and bottom two marks from the average to reduce the risk of partisan or malicious marking. Peer marking will mean the students examine all the efforts with a more thoughtful eye, and learn a lot more. Having to assess others is one of the most powerful forces to developing greater understanding of a subject.

Work experience is one area where mixed media stands are a good form of 'reporting back'. Visualising and preparing such a stand during the work experience can help sharpen students' analysis of their experience. But there must be a thesis like "I learned how to work as a member of a team" or "It was hard to discipline myself to the routine". The thesis may not emerge until towards the end of work experience so it is important to tell the students to cover a lot of angles - interviews with employees, videos of work in action, documents, keeping a journal, and generally amassing material of all kinds.

It is also important to give the students some advice on using audiovisual media, and on communication skills in this context. You could have some 'guest' sessions beforehand with someone from Communication Studies, Media Studies, and from Media Services to give practical advice.

You can probably think of a range of similar ways in which mixed media can be used in project work. Instead of stands, students could prepare portfolios, for example.

Group Seminars:

The students make individual presentations as a part of a group presentation on a given theme. You are looking for good teamwork as well as good content and use of media. You can make it a requirement that students use the OHP, make slides, use a 'found' piece of video etc. Again peer assessment is a good driver

Figure 9: Presentation Assessment Sheet

Name of Assessor: --- Date: ----------------

Title of Presentation: ---

Scale: Good   Fair   Poor

   5   4   3   2   1

Criterion	Score
Statement of Purpose and Thesis	
Relevance of Resources to Purpose	
Coherence (i.e. resources well related)	
Variety of Resources	
Effectiveness of Communication	
Originality of Materials/Approach	
Quality of Resources (e.g. well made)	
Presentation of Resources	
Interest Generated	
Overall Assessment	
Total/50	